SIDEHUSTLE MILLIONAIRE

How to Build a Side Business That Creates Financial Freedom

BY

TONY WHATLEY

Ordering Information:
Quantity sales. Special discounts are available on quantity purchases by corporations, associations, and others. Orders by U.S. trade bookstores and wholesalers. Please contact TONY WHATLEY via www.365Driven.com

Edited and Marketed By
DreamStarters University
www.DreamStartersUniversity.com

CONTENTS

DEDICATION

This book is dedicated to all the people who have positively influenced my life. To those who have supported me unconditionally, even when my dreams seemed outrageous.

This book is also dedicated to each of you that finds the message within it, and are driven to pursue your potential. I can't wait to meet you.

Dreams can come true, but only by taking action!

INTRODUCTION

Who is this book for?

This book is for the self-motivated individual who simply wants more than what his or her current career path offers. You may have already invested years of your time and thousands of dollars into your career. Perhaps you already have a college degree, specialized training, or certifications. You view these as personal investments you've made, and find it difficult to simply walk away from them. You don't necessarily dislike what you do. You may even love what you do. You may have even reached what most would consider a high level of income. But, you have come to the realization that your career path does not lead to the financial success or quality of life you wish to have. You could just be craving a creative outlet, or wanting to do something to enhance your leadership skills. Maybe you'd like to have a hobby that pays for itself. You may just feel like you are operating nowhere near your potential.

Welcome to the side-hustle. No doubt you've heard this catchy phrase. It is a play on the popular word "hustle" that gets tossed around on social media and in numerous entrepreneurship teachings. The side-hustle is exactly what the name implies; it is a business that you operate on the side. The good news? You do not have to quit your job or discard your financial safety net.

My goal is to help you master the mindset and methods that I have personally used to create multiple businesses and generate astounding income levels.

Who is the author?

I'm Tony Whatley. I grew up in a small town outside of Houston, Texas. My dad is a veteran U.S. Marine that served in the Vietnam War. After the military, he worked his way up through the blue-collar ranks of the Houston area refineries. My mom spent her entire career serving meals to children as a cafeteria lady in the public school system. My dad instilled in me his values of integrity, toughness and leadership. My mom taught me empathy for others, creativity and patience. Both of my parents taught me that life isn't fair, and that I'd have to work for whatever I wanted in life.

I put myself through college while working full-time as a pipefitter and welder, attending school at night. On weekends, I also worked in restaurants to help pay bills. It took me seven years to earn a degree in mechanical engineering. Those were tough years. I was severely in debt and struggled to keep up. I only slept about four hours per night. My grades and relationships suffered. But, I never quit.

I've held a fascinating career in oil and gas since I was 18. Having started in the field, I later began working my way through engineering design roles and then made my way into project management. I've worked overseas in Europe, as well as in Africa. I enjoy the innovation, challenge, and complexity of managing $100M+ large-scale projects. I thrive in these leadership roles. By several measures, I've led a successful and highly-paid corporate career.

But, having a corporate career was never enough for me. I wanted a creative outlet, more responsibilities, and some padding for added financial stability. Alongside my oil career, I slowly became an expert at creating side-hustle businesses. I've started a few businesses that have generated incredible income with minimal time requirements. Once these businesses were set up, I've managed them in only 1-2 hours per day. One of these side businesses generated multiple six-figures of yearly profit, far more than my oil career at the time. In 2007, at age 34, I became a millionaire when a business partner and I sold our company for multiple 7-figures. All of this was accomplished in our spare time, a true side-hustle business for each of us.

A few years ago, I began to ponder my main purpose in life. I've always enjoyed teaching, so I decided that I wanted to teach others how to become the best version of themselves. I want to help businesses become more successful. I truly enjoy helping those who are willing to learn, those willing to take action. Your success is how I define my success. In the past, I never had any formal mentors to discuss my business and success goals with. I only had hundreds of books and people that I admired. I learned by trial and error, and I failed plenty of times along the way. Although I've accomplished much, I now realize that I could have progressed much faster if I had utilized mentors and coaches, people who had accomplished the things that I desired to achieve—mentors who would help me focus, create a strategy, and hold me accountable.

This is why I wrote this book. I look forward to helping you.

More of my story and personal experiences can be found in the final chapter of this book.

CHAPTER 1

ENTREPRENEUR

What do you think of when you hear the word "entrepreneur"? Do popular names immediately come to mind such as Bezos, Musk, or Zuckerberg? Do you perceive this title as something to aspire to? It almost seems like a very cool and exclusive club membership. It is a way to tell the world that you are a confident risk-taker that bets on yourself. It says that you are in control of your own destiny.

Social media, print, and television have sensationalized and glamourized the successful entrepreneur. They have elevated the perceived social status of those whom were once simply called "business owners." There are thousands of celebrities and professional athletes who have also taken on the title of entrepreneur later in their careers. We are almost confronted daily with motivational images that say things such as, "No Risk, No Reward."

The cold, hard truth is that being an entrepreneur is hard. It takes dedication, discipline, and putting in the work. There is no "get-rich-quick." That simply doesn't exist. While we may be fascinated with the success stories, we rarely hear about the numerous failure stories. 20% of new businesses fail within the first year, according to the US Bureau of Labor

Statistics. At the five year mark, only 50% of those businesses still remain open. There are far more failure stories out there than there are success stories. Starting a full-time business is a risky proposition. The statistics do not lie.

Knowing the failure rate, we must look for ways to reduce risk. I find no honor in recommending that you push some sort of career reset button and quit your job to become an entrepreneur. This would be like jumping out of a flying airplane without a parachute on. With proper control of a parachute, you can control where you land, and you will eventually arrive at your personal goal. Once you arrive safely on the ground, then it may make sense to remove the career parachute and take on the business full-time. Or, perhaps you might continue to run it as a side business indefinitely, as a supplemental income source. It could be something that generates passive income, or maybe even something that safeguards you against downturns in your career.

We all have financial obligations to ourselves and to our families. I suggest to my clients that they attempt to earn the most income possible in the most efficient manner possible. If you can earn six-figures from your normal career, it may not make financial sense to earn less doing your own business just to claim you are an entrepreneur. If at some point your side-hustle begins to take off and can replace your career income, wait until then to re-evaluate the arrangement. There was a time that my side-hustle business was generating more annual income than my engineering career, but I had the time to do both. Some would have quit their normal job, but my side-hustle was only requiring about 1-2 hours per day of my time. The business wasn't a distraction, and I could more than double my income by operating both concurrently. This was simply making efficient use of my time to maximize my income.

Side-Hustlers & Solopreneurs

You may have already done some initial research on the world of side-hustle businesses. There are numerous podcasts, blogs, books and videos on this subject. There is no shortage of ideas or opinions available. But, I feel it is important to share my viewpoint on this popular niche of side-businesses. This way you can see the foundation my decision-making comes from.

I feel the majority of the side-hustle business community sets goals far too low. Worse yet, they don't set goals at all. I find that most businesses are built around providing a product or service that doesn't consider future business expansion, growth or scalability. Many of the markets people get into consume a lot of their time and produce minimal profit. Just because a business is considered part-time, that doesn't necessarily mean you should limit yourself to part-time levels of income. Your time is what is valuable. We never get a refund on the time we have spent.

This ties back into my previous statement of earning the most income possible in the most efficient manner possible. If your financial goals are just to earn a couple hundred bucks extra per month, you can do this very easily. If you eventually want to replace your career income, picking the right business model is vital. Let's say that you are considering two different business ideas to start. Both require the same time commitment from you, but one idea has far greater potential. Would you rather earn $300 extra per month or $30,000 extra per month? The choice is yours, but I prefer to earn far more for my time. It is my goal to teach you this mindset, even if you still decide to choose smaller goals afterwards. At the very least, this mindset will raise financial awareness about your business ideas.

Summary Chapter 1

•   The title of "Entrepreneur" can be a source of pride, and is something that's admired by others.
•   There is no such thing as "get-rich-quick." Being an entrepreneur is hard, and it takes work.
•   About 20% of businesses fail in the first year. By five years, about 50% of those remaining have also closed.
•   You must learn to identify, calculate, and mitigate risk.
•   Most business owners start with goals set too low. Set them high!
•   Consider your time. Would you prefer to earn more or less for the same amount of time?

Recommended Reading

•   *Crushing It* by Gary Vaynerchuk
•   *The 5 Second Rule* by Mel Robbins
•   *The School of Greatness* by Lewis Howes
•   *The 4-Hour Work-Week* by Timothy Ferriss
•   *Awaken The Giant Within* by Tony Robbins

"Many of life's failures are people who did not realize how close they were to success when they gave up."

Thomas Edison, Inventor

CHAPTER 2
MINDSET

Before you head down the path of creating your own business, you must first work on the most important aspect of business ownership: your mindset. This will take some strong self-awareness, and you have to be honest with yourself. Lying to yourself serves no purpose. Unlike other business startup books, I will be spending far more time on the mindset, behaviors, and habits of successful people in this book. This subject is vital, and this will likely be the most important chapter of this book. Your mindset serves as the foundation on which your company gets built, and it determines if it will succeed.

Conquer the Excuses

There is no shortage of excuses available when it comes to the consideration of starting a new business. Many people have simply created mental roadblocks and set self-imposed limits on their own potential. Most of us already know the answers to our hardest questions, yet we still seek validation from others to take that first step. The internal struggle is the real battle here, and nothing more.

While gathering research data for this book, I sent out a series of questions to my social media network. I received over 100 responses back from a group that consists of current business owners and aspiring entrepreneurs. There was no specific industry requirement, no age or gender bias, nor business revenue target. I received feedback from at least five different countries as well. This effort was purely to discover the main reasons that people do not start their first business and to identify the main drivers to starting a business. While I had their valuable attention, I also asked people what lessons they've learned, what challenges they've faced, and what changes they would make if they were to start all over again. The data below is expressed in a percentage based on the number of responses received. I removed any single-digit responses to provide more focus on the predominant replies.

What were the top 3 reasons that kept you from, or delayed you from starting a business?

- 58%   Fear, self-doubt, lack of confidence
- 56%   Lack of money or funding
- 36%   Lack of knowledge, experience, or education
- 33%   Already had comfortable salary / benefits
- 25%   Lack of time
- 25%   Too many ideas, lack of focus
- 18%   Negative influence from friends or family

Fear is Imaginary

Fear is the number one reason that most people do not attempt to do something. Respondents to the questionnaire mentioned the fear of failure, fear of rejection, and some even mentioned the fear of becoming successful. You can come up with a myriad of other surface-level excuses, but many of them stem from simply being afraid. This is the difference between having a fixed mindset versus a growth mindset. Here is the secret that few seem to discuss openly when it comes to chasing success: Failure is part of the process. Failure should be avoided when possible, but it should also be expected. There are only two outcomes from an attempt at anything; you either win – or you learn. Think back to all the failures you've experienced in your life. Did you learn something from those? Absolutely. The sooner that you reframe failure as part of the process to achieving success, and accept that it sometimes happens, the sooner you will be willing to take the leap. Stop avoiding the pain of effort, and accepting the pain of regret. Pain is temporary. Regret lasts forever.

Are you worried about what other people will say if you fail? Throw that nonsense out the window. Put their comments into context. Have any of them accomplished what you desire to accomplish? Have any of them been brave enough to step into the same arena as you? It is more honorable to have tried and failed than to have never tried at all.

Fear is imaginary. It is intangible, and you can't put your hands on it. It is purely a mental roadblock, which you will need to put in serious effort to improve upon. It is unfortunate that so many people are held back from reaching their potential simply because of a lack of self-confidence. Confidence is purely a decision. It isn't a genetic characteristic. You simply have to decide to be confident, even if it feels uncomfortable at first. This is how you build real confidence, by trying it more often. If you want to change something in your life, you must decide to step out of your comfort zone, and take action. You can never expect change without first changing yourself in the process. Instead of focusing so much on "What if I fail?", consider reframing that mindset into "What if I succeed?" What would your life look like if you were to succeed? Focus on that.

No Money

Lack of money was near the top, as expected. However, many of these business owners mentioned that the money excuse was mostly a figment of their imagination prior to getting started. Once they actually started the company, they realized how inexpensive it can be to actually start a business. Not every business requires huge funding. Many can be started for a few hundred bucks. So, before you put money as a reason not to start, be sure to evaluate if the business you want to start actually requires a large investment. You may find it doesn't. With e-commerce websites such as Amazon, eBay, and Shopify, you can literally set up an online retail business with minimal effort and no knowledge of website creation.

While there are certainly well-known companies that started with millions invested, the fact is that there are also millions of companies that were started with little to no money invested. The company that I earned the most from only cost $350 to start. Six years later, it sold for millions. While this example is certainly an exception, the potential still exists. Other people have sold startup companies for billions in shorter amounts of time. Money should never be your excuse for not starting a business, it should just motivate you to solve the root problem – how to get more money. You can use crowdfunding, borrow from banks, friends, or family. You can choose to bootstrap fund it by working extra jobs, reducing unnecessary expenses, or by selling some possessions. There are numerous ways to solve money issues that all involve some sort of sacrifice. If this business is important to you, then you simply need to prioritize your expenses. If you lack money, trade your time for more money. You may even decide to start a simple side-hustle business or service just to save up more money to parlay that savings into a different business later. Your dream business may just become possible after you've built and sold a few smaller businesses along the way.

I Don't Know Enough

Feeling as if you do not have enough experience or knowledge is also similar to lack of money in one way. It is only a perceived roadblock, as many entrepreneurs discovered that they were able to start and just learn as they go. The truth is, we never stop learning. Learning isn't something we "did." It is something we "do."

Lack of knowledge is a weak excuse, especially for anyone that has access to a smartphone and the internet. The world is literally at your fingertips. You can teach yourself anything you want by reading books or blogs, listening to books or podcasts, finding a mentor, joining a Facebook group on the subject, watching YouTube videos, and the like. There is no shortage of information available 24 hours per day. This excuse may have been more valid in 1999, but it simply doesn't apply today.

Some of the most successful people I personally know do not have a formal education. Some were high school drop-outs. Some even have learning disabilities like ADHD or dyslexia. These people became self-made multi-millionaires.

You've no doubt heard numerous stories that are similar. You may even know a few people like this. Education or knowledge is a minor barrier, which is easy to overcome. You have to decide to learn something. Picking up this book proves you are committed to doing so.

Don't stop with just this book. Consume all sorts of knowledge that will help you achieve your goals. Think of this book as just the baseline, the starting point. Once I discovered free podcasts and audiobooks, it opened up a world of potential mentors and thought leaders on every conceivable subject. I prefer audiobooks and podcasts because I can listen while I do other daily routines. You can listen while driving or commuting, during exercise, and during meals. You may find you have a few hours per day to increase your knowledge just by putting on a pair of earphones. Most audiobooks only take about 6-8 hours total to listen to. The same book might take months for you to finish by reading, because you can't read while doing other things. The $10-15 you typically spend on a book is worthwhile if you just learn one thing from it.

No Time

People love to tell other people that they are "too busy" to add more activities to their plate. Saying you "don't have time" is just the socially acceptable excuse for saying that something is not a priority to you. The truth is that we always make time for our priorities, no matter what they may be. It is purely your choice, your decision, to make something a priority. The things you are doing now are your priority. You just haven't felt enough pain yet in order to shift priorities. Make a list of all the small things that take place in your daily routine to see where you could be wasting precious time.

Could you do things more efficiently to help get some of that time back? Are there distractions that you are willing to give up to focus on your business? In today's digital business landscape, you may only need 10 minutes per day to keep a business operating once it is established. This is entirely possible.

For those who claim they are waiting for the right time to start, here is the harsh reality: There will never be a right time to start. The perfect time is right now! The excuses that you are using to keep yourself from starting today will just be replaced with a different group of excuses tomorrow. This will never end unless you break that cycle.

In this book, you will learn to divide and prioritize individual tasks to form a complete process. When you know exactly which next step to take, you won't focus on the entire project as a whole. You'll learn to execute each step in order. Once you learn to prioritize your tasks, you will then be able to focus on the most important task each day. This is the single task that moves you the furthest towards your goal. This task is also typically the one that causes you to feel the most anxiety or pain. The painful tasks have an uncanny way of being the priority tasks. Don't run from these priorities. Face them head on and get them over with. Distracting yourself with other less important tasks may make you fool yourself into thinking you are busy, but being busy is not the same thing as being productive. You must learn to politely say NO to distractions. One of the resounding statements that we hear in leadership courses is this: Work on the problems that you should work on, not the problems that you want to work on.

Squirrel Syndrome

Have you ever observed an unleashed dog at a park? They go nuts at the sight of a squirrel and run their legs off in hot pursuit of the bushy-tailed rodent. That is, until they see another squirrel, which causes them to change direction and go hard-charging after the newest target. Repeat this enough times, and we all know the outcome. They never catch a squirrel, and even if they did – they wouldn't know what to do with one. Quit chasing squirrels or "shiny objects" in your life.

This is a lack of focus issue. You are not alone when it comes to having numerous ideas for products or services to offer to the world. Ideas are the easy part, so don't pat yourself on the back for having a bunch of creative ideas. Ideas are worthless unless you take action to execute them.

You may also be suffering from "analysis paralysis," which is when you overthink everything so much that you become paralyzed and fearful to take further action. Starting and operating a company seems overwhelming when you take a moment to think about everything required to do so as a complete project. It certainly looks overwhelming when you think of every single aspect of a business as a huge mountain of tasks. I even suffered from this same paralysis when it came to writing this book. I've never written a book or published anything before. The idea for this book was in my mind for a couple years. I even had an outline for the rough draft already completed a year before I began typing. But, I always hesitated to begin until I trusted the process. Later in this book, I will cover how to quickly evaluate your ideas, gain focus, and set priorities. You've found the right resource.

Circle of Friends & Family

I address this topic quite often with my clients—the influencing power of your inner circle of friends and family.

People love to keep relationships and attachments, even if they are negative or caustic. It is difficult for some people to let go, and they try to please everyone. If you are not being supported within your circle, it is time to find a better circle. Spend less time with those who hold you back, and replace them with people that encourage and support you. If you need further proof that this is a good idea, ask every single successful person you know how important this is.

Many times, negative circles can also alter your perception of successful people. Our politics and news media outlets have historically been very purposeful about engaging in economic division. We constantly hear about the groupings of "poverty class, middle class, upper class." This class mindset makes the majority of people feel stuck within a specific class, and this can diminish their hopes of ever upgrading financial classes. You may have even had parents, family, or friends that influenced you into thinking all rich people are unethical.

You may come from a background where discussing money is considered taboo, and you may believe that you shouldn't talk about it with other people. This could result in a negative perception of success and an underlying fear of having others judge you if you become successful. How will you ever earn money if you are afraid to even talk about it? In order to succeed, you have to make yourself comfortable with being uncomfortable. Gain knowledge in any subject, and you will gain confidence in discussing that subject.

Take a look at the source of your negative idea of money, and put things into context. You will find that successful people, who are more comfortable with discussing money, are unlikely to hold the view that other successful people are all bad. I've found that when you surround yourself with other successful people, they tend to lift each other up, not talk each other down. Successful people understand that there is no shortage of opportunity for success. There is plenty to go around.

Loser mindset people think that if someone else gains more success, somehow they lose some success. Loser mindset people express jealousy and hatred for those who have more than them. They see the final results of a successful person, but never acknowledge the struggle it took to reach that level. It requires effort for them to improve and become disciplined, but it takes nothing for them to hate. I grew up without money, and I was fortunate to have parents that wanted me to dream and to achieve great things. I never heard them disparage anyone, especially about their financial standing. I grew up watching the amount of effort and work that it took for my parents to pay the bills. I understood that money was a positive thing.

Personally, I feel it is your duty to earn to your potential. What you do with the excess money is up to you. If you are into philanthropy, you can donate the excess. If you want to increase the quality of your lifestyle, you can spend the excess in numerous ways. I want everyone to be as successful as they can possibly be.

Having extra money is just a way of having more options in life available to you. I've been broke and severely in debt before. I had no options except for doing more work. I worked three jobs and did whatever I could to dig myself out of that deep hole. It was a very low point in my life, but I never gave up. I put my head down, and I got to work. It took me three years to get back to zero. That is right—zero!

We have all heard the popular statement that "Money does not buy happiness." I agree wholeheartedly with this statement. I've known several people in my lifetime that went from broke to rich, and others that went from rich to broke. Income level does not change attitude or demeanor. If you are optimistic and happy when you are broke, you'll also be happy when you are rich. If you are negative and pessimistic when you are broke, you'll also be negative when you are rich. There isn't a direct relationship between money and happiness. That is an individual character issue. There are plenty of other books and doctors that can help you find your happiness. If you find that your circle of friends and family keep surrounding you with negative mindsets, you must move on.

Reasons to Start

Now that we've covered all the popular excuses for not starting a business, let's take a look into the popular reasons why people do start businesses.

What were your top 3 reasons to start a business?
- 82%   To create independence or flexibility
- 73%   Increase of income
- 35%   Gain a sense of personal accomplishment
- 24%   Following passion, fun, or enjoyment
- 20%   To help other people, or build a legacy

Freedom! There was certainly a breakaway response within this pack of responses. While the potential increase in income was important to most, the idea of being in control of their own destiny was the most important reason to start a business. How many of these resonate with you?

In regards to your side-hustle business, what reasons keep you from quitting your normal career?

- 49%   Need for steady income or benefits
- 20%   They enjoy their current career

The funny thing about this question is that I did not request any specific amount of reasons. But, we ended up with basically two reasons that people would start a side-hustle business, rather than focus on making it a full-time business. People said they simply could not walk away from the financial stability their 9-5 job offers. Some even love their current job. They just want to increase income on the side. Does this sound familiar?

Once your business was started, what were your 3 most difficult challenges about running the business?
- 40%   Managing cash flow, financial and taxes
- 31%   Lack of salesmanship or marketing skill
- 29%   Managing partners, employees, contractors
- 20%   Time management
- 16%   Managing growth or expansion
- 11%   Work / Life balance

The number one reason businesses fail is cash flow. Some online studies suggest as much as 80% of failed businesses are directly related to cash flow problems. Money is the lifeblood of your company, and it is essential for you to manage it properly. You should make financials the #1 responsibility in your business, because you cannot operate without money. As a business consultant, I can't count how many times I've seen small businesses fail because they got behind on bills and tried to drum up new business to pay for old debts. This always leaves the last round of customers screwed when the doors eventually shut on the business. Get ahead of that. Be sure to keep enough cash on hand to operate your business, and flow that money through the process properly. Make sure you are collecting on money owed to you!

Marketing and selling seem to be really weak skills for many new business owners. Pay extra attention to this! Just because you are a technical wizard, or have some awesome talent or knowledge in a niche, this doesn't make you good at selling. This is Business 101—your business must exist to create a financial transaction. Too many people jump into starting a business, but have no clue on how to advertise, capture leads, or close a deal. There are numerous books, courses, and coaches out there that can help you with this. Do not take this lack of skill lightly!

Has your business achieved your original goals?
- 47%   Not met goals
- 22%   Exceeded goals
- 13%   Met goals

This feedback shows us the hard truth. Not every company is successful in the eyes of the owner. I know that it seems trendy for people to want to become entrepreneurs, but the reality is that there is still a lot of work required. Many times, we are buried under trivial tasks that we should be delegating or outsourcing, and we do not accomplish the priority tasks. There are many important aspects to running a business, and many times you feel like you are just trying to coordinate chaos. We spend too much time trying to fix our personal weaknesses, rather than hiring others who will complement our strengths.

If you could do things all over again, what would you do differently?
- 31%   Would have started sooner

- • 15%   Find coach, accountability partner, or mentor
- • 11%   Been more focused on the core business

I received numerous responses to this open-ended question, but these are the only three that got into double-digits of responses.

Starting sooner was certainly the most common response, and this should help encourage you to take that first step. There is a Chinese proverb that I enjoy thinking about that goes like this: "The best time to plant a tree was 20 years ago. The second best time is today." Those who responded wishing they had started sooner, no doubt feel this tree proverb in their mind. They can imagine where they would be today had they started growing their business sooner.

The second most popular response was simply asking others for help. Even though we always hear successful people recommend finding a mentor or coach, it seems too many of us put this task aside. We allow our pride, ego, or anxiety to hold us back from asking for advice from others. Those who have done what you want to do, can save you years, if not decades of time. You will learn about their failures and how to avoid them. You will learn about their strategies for growth and how to implement them. I've also been guilty of not asking for help or advice while trying to feed a false sense of pride that I did everything myself. I now understand how much more I could have accomplished had I used mentors sooner. You see, even a business consultant and coach still needs a mentor! Never be afraid to ask for help. Just be respectful of other people's time. And never hesitate to help others when called upon.

I hope this research data has been useful for your mental processing of when and why to start. I hope it shows you that the fears and thoughts you currently have are common, and that you aren't alone. Hopefully this will help reduce your fears, and even encourage your bravery.

Summary Chapter 2

- Your mindset serves as the foundation on which your company gets built, and it determines if it succeeds.
- Fear and confidence are both imaginary. You simply decide which one to live with.
- If you don't have the money to start your dream business, perhaps you should start a different business to build up and sell, and then use the money you earn from selling it to buy your dream business.
- Lack of knowledge is a weak excuse considering the knowledge available on the internet and in podcasts, books, and videos. You can truly learn anything you want.
- Saying "I don't have time" is the exact same thing as saying "It isn't my priority." We always make time for our priorities. The things you are doing now are your priorities.
- Business ideas are the easy part. Don't give yourself too much credit for having ideas. They are worthless unless you take action on them.
- Your circle of influence matters. Distance yourself from naysayers, haters, and those who do not support your dream. Find new networks that encourage and support you.
- The main reason businesses fail is poor cash flow management. This results in about 80% of all business failures.

Recommended Reading

- *The 10X Rule* by Grant Cardone
- *The Success Principles* by Jack Canfield
- *Relentless* by Tim Grover
- *Extreme Ownership* by Jocko Willink

- *The Alchemist* by Paulo Coelho
- *Daring Greatly* by Brené Brown
- *The One Thing* by Gary Keller & Jay Papasan

"Successful and unsuccessful people do not vary greatly in their abilities. They vary in their desires to reach their potential."

Lewis Howes, Entrepreneur, Best-Selling Author

CHAPTER 3

IDEAS

The most difficult question for an aspiring entrepreneur is where to start. First, you need an idea for a product or service that you could earn income with. Even better, have several ideas to choose from. I see so many people failing at business because they start with the wrong purpose. I can't count how many of my contacts have bought into get-rich-quick type schemes or pursued specific industries only for the money potential. They fail because their heart simply isn't into the subject matter. They lose interest quickly, or they get distracted by the next shiny business idea. If your sole purpose is to earn money, be sure that the business or product at least interests you. I always recommend that someone follow their passions, and start a business based on something that they love. Money typically follows passion. When you work within your passions, you are less likely to give up and more likely to push towards success. You also tend to continually invest in yourself with education and training to master your passion subject. Your passions can be identified with one simple question: If you could do one thing every day for the rest of your life, and get paid for it, what would that be?

Let's disregard the wisecrack answers of "semi-pro beer drinker" or "TV show binge-watching expert." You still have to be realistic with your definition of your passions. Is the subject within your skill set or knowledge capability? Not everyone can be an Olympic gold medalist or disprove quantum physics theories. Some level of self-awareness is certainly required. You also have to come up with a method to earn income from the idea, somehow.

Everyone in the world has plenty of ideas. Ideas are the easy part. Every single day, thousands of people die with great ideas that never get shared with the world. Each of us can probably sit down and brainstorm at least ten ideas for businesses to start based on products or services. But, ideas are absolutely worthless unless you take action on them.

Within this chapter, I will share how to quickly evaluate each of your ideas with a simple process. This is an important step to master so that you do not waste time or money chasing weak or risky ideas. I've made numerous mistakes during my entrepreneurial journey. I've discovered roadblocks and dead ends along the way, even some that I never considered. I want to help you navigate around those costly mishaps, and learn from my mistakes.

Business Language

If you are a new to the business world, do not let financial or business terminology scare you. The definitions are pretty simple, and each is important to understand. I'd even suggest you watch a full season of Shark Tank if you want to get a grasp of how these terms are used.

Let's introduce some common business terms so that you can think and speak in a financial sense. It is very important that you master these terms, regardless of which business you pursue. Those who aren't fluent in discussing business could get taken advantage of by those who are.

Revenue – The total amount of income your business receives from all sales within a specified time period. Also known as "gross income" and sometimes called the "top line."
Expenses – This is the total of all of the true costs of operating your business. Raw materials needed to build products, employee salaries, building lease cost, shipping/freight, utilities, taxes, marketing and advertising, and any other costs. This is also known as "overhead."
Profit – This is what your company actually earns within a specified time period. It is what remains after you subtract all the expenses from the revenue. This is also known as the "bottom line", since it is the last line on a financial statement.
Margin – The ratio between your business' revenue vs. expenses. Divide the profit by the revenue and multiply that answer by 100 to get the margin percentage value. Margin can also refer to products or services. It is the ratio between the costs to create a product vs. the price which it is sold for. The formulas for margin are:

For a business:
$$\text{Margin} = (\text{Profit} / \text{Revenue})$$

For an individual product or service:
$$\text{Margin} = (\text{Price} - \text{Cost}) / \text{Price}$$

Multiply each of these margin values by 100 to arrive at the % value, which is generally how they are stated.

Brainstorm Ideas

Let's do an exercise together. Take out a blank piece of paper, grab a pen and turn on your imagination.
• Write down every single idea for a product or service that you may be even remotely interested in offering.
• If you have any skills, knowledge, or talents that could be monetized, write those down.
• What are your hobbies and passions? Write down business ideas that relate to those.
• Think of some ordinary problems that you face during your daily routine or while at work. Can you come up with solutions to those problems? Write them down.
• Keep writing down ideas, no matter how small or how crazy they may seem.

Keep writing until you can no longer think of anything else to add. You may even ask friends or family to participate in this brainstorm session to help identify other things that you could have possibly missed. Maybe they might recognize other strengths in you, which you may not notice. They may even have suggestions for businesses that they think you could be great at based on your skill set, knowledge, and personality.

The best side-hustles are based on skills, knowledge or resources that you already have. Or, ideas that require very little time for you to learn and implement. Sure, it sounds like a dream to create a phone app that sells for a billion dollars to Google, but if you don't know how to build or program an app, it could take you years to learn how to do so. There is no easy way to success. There are only the right ways. If your dream invention consists of a product that requires extensive design, engineering and millions invested to produce…but you don't have the knowledge or resources to accomplish it, then it may not be a good idea for you. This is when you must practice self-awareness and utilize your current skills and strengths. Doing so will always help you to start creating income sooner.

Initial Evaluation

Start with the end in mind. You may be thinking, "What? How could I possibly know the end goal of my business? I haven't even started it yet." Don't worry, I'm not crazy, and neither are you. Nobody is certain of where their business can take them, but we can certainly define some personal goals based on money.

With your new list of potential business ideas in front of you, it is now time to evaluate each of them individually. Before you do this, you must first define your short-term and long-term profit goals. I recommend 1 year, 5 year, and 10 year profit goals. Think of measurable, actual dollar values. Saying "I want to be rich" is not a measurable goal. There is no dollar value to measure against, and "rich" is a subjective description. Better examples of measurable goals are "I want to earn $200,000 per year" or "I would like to earn $5 million in 10 years." Both of these are good, specific goals, as there is a dollar value and a time value in each. This makes them measurable. You will know when you achieve these goals. I do not typically recommend setting just attainable, easy goals. I usually recommend aiming higher, as larger goals are more likely to motivate you and keep you motivated. When people set goals too low, they become complacent, lazy, and content.

With your defined profit goals in mind, you can then calculate the yearly revenue required to achieve that goal.

This exercise will also test the validity and likelihood of each business idea to achieve the income level of your goals.

Here is an example calculation. Let's say you want to open a new business, and your financial goal is to earn $200,000 profit per year. You then do some Google research on this type of business niche to find the typical industry margin for similar businesses. This margin may also vary based on your geographical location. Let's assume you discover that your business idea usually has an average of 20% margin (or 0.20).

For a small business, the simple calculation is:
Revenue = Profit / Margin
Revenue = $200,000 / 0.20
Revenue = $1,000,000

This simple calculation tells you that in order to earn $200,000 profit per year at a 20% margin, you would need to have a sales revenue of $1,000,000 in products or services per year.

This quick calculation will likely tell you if your business idea is a waste of time, or if the idea needs to be further refined to improve the potential. Does it seem realistic or possible to achieve the calculated sales revenue to reach your profit goal? Keep in mind that anything you can do to increase the margin value or increase revenue will also increase profit. Perhaps your business idea isn't easily scalable for growth, or maybe your potential customer base is too small. Maybe the business expenses are simply too high or product margins are too low, which adversely affects the business profit. By doing these calculations, you will find that many of your ideas do not align with the financial goals you have. Do not be discouraged, because this is quite common. You must be willing to accept the harsh reality of each of your business ideas. Some will have the potential to meet your goals, and others will not. Your choice is either to reduce your financial goals, figure out how to increase sales revenue, or think of some better business ideas. Don't waste a minute chasing an idea that will never arrive at the goals you have set. Create, plan, and execute only the best ideas to potentially reach your goals. Let's visualize what it takes to earn one million dollars in revenue.

One Million Dollars?

Following our previous revenue calculation example, you may be wondering how to create annual revenue of one million dollars. There are several ways to reach that final amount. Whenever you are considering products or services to sell, think of these scenarios and see which one may actually work for your business model.

$1,000,000 Revenue =
Sell a $1 product to 1 million people
Sell a $10 product to 100,000 people
Sell a $1,000 product to 1,000 people
Sell a $10,000 product to 100 people
Sell a $100,000 product to 10 people
Sell a $1,000,000 product to 1 person

Detailed Evaluation

After you have completed the initial evaluation of your business ideas, and filtered your list down to the remaining potential choices, we can look into each with more detail.

There are many factors and variables that can contribute to the success of a business. This deeper evaluation will begin to scrape away at the surface idea, and possibly uncover several aspects or risks that you may have not considered yet.

Looking at the remaining ideas you may have, rate them in terms of your interest or motivation level. Rate them on a scale of 1 to 5, with 1 being the worst and 5 being the best.

Your Motivation & Interest

Business Idea A	1	2	3	**4**	5
Business Idea B	1	**2**	3	4	5
Business Idea C	1	2	**3**	4	5

Next, rate each business in terms of profit potential.

Profit Potential

Business Idea A	1	2	**3**	4	5
Business Idea B	1	2	3	**4**	5
Business Idea C	1	2	3	4	**5**

Next, rate each business in terms of the efficiency of which you could get each started sooner. This is to determine how much knowledge, equipment, money, or other resources you already have available to start up each idea.

Efficiency to Start Up

Business Idea A	1	2	3	4	**5**
Business Idea B	1	2	**3**	4	5
Business Idea C	1	2	**3**	4	5

With this simple little comparison test, we can use simple math addition to rate each of these ideas. Knowing that a higher total value means a better rating, we can assess the following:

Business Idea A
>4 Motivation & Interest
>3 Profit Potential
>5 Efficiency

Total = 4+3+5 = 12

Business Idea B
>2 Motivation & Interest
>4 Profit Potential
>3 Efficiency

Total = 2+4+3 = 9

Business Idea C
>3 Motivation & Interest
>5 Profit Potential
>3 Efficiency

Total = 3+5+3 = 11

From this simple quantitative comparison, it seems that Idea A may present the best odds at success, as it has the highest (most desirable) total. This is just one way to compare several of your ideas, at the same time.

Simple Business Plan

Putting together a business plan doesn't have to be that complicated, especially if you aren't seeking a bank loan. It is essentially a summary of all the costs and expenses that you can think of compared to your hopeful projected sales revenue. Comparing costs vs. revenue is how you forecast your profit. You can do this on a spreadsheet program rather quickly, or with just a piece of paper and a pen.

Make two columns on the page. The left column will represent your monthly expenses and costs. The right column will represent your monthly revenue received from sales.

Calculate Monthly Costs & Expenses

Within the left column, write down every single thing you can think of that will cost money each month. Do your best to estimate these, or do some research to find these costs in your area.

Here are some examples:

Office/property mortgage or rent
Property maintenance
State and federal taxes
Bank loans
Employee 1 salary
Employee 2 salary, etc.
Professional services
Electricity bill
Water bill
Phone bill
Internet bill
Waste bill
Shipping / postage costs
Computer / licenses
Insurance / legal
Advertising / marketing
Cost of goods / products
Office supplies

Security
Travel / entertainment expenses
Vehicle / mileage expenses

Also, for a startup, you will have to capture and budget for some one-time expenses in the first month. Examples are:

Office build-out or remodel
Furniture & electronics
Equipment costs
Shelving & storage
Signage & stationary
Graphic design for logo
Website development
Uniforms
Business registration fees
Initial inventory

Calculate Monthly Sales Revenue

Now that all of the costs have been captured, move on to the right column and calculate the revenue that will be generated by the business. If your business is based on hired services, you can use the hourly rate for each employee to calculate potential revenue. Use your estimated target revenue from the initial evaluation exercises performed earlier. You have already captured the costs for your products in the left column, so on the right side you should only capture the total sales received from these products. Here is an example of how to calculate the revenue from a service employee, such as a mechanic.

Your customer is charged $80/hour to pay for the mechanic's labor. At 40 hours per week, times an average of 4.35 weeks per month, the calculation of monthly revenue for one mechanic is:

Revenue = $80 x 40 x 4.35
Revenue = $13,920 per month

To calculate your total sales revenue on products, simply estimate the quantity of each item you hope to sell multiplied by the price for each item. Here is an example:

Revenue = 100 items sold at $46 each
Revenue = $4,600 per month

Calculate Monthly Profit

Now that you have a list of monthly expenses and monthly revenue, you can calculate your monthly profit. Simply subtract the expenses from the revenue.

Profit = Revenue – Expenses

If the profit is a positive value, congrats! This means you can actually earn money with the business. If the profit comes out as a negative value, that means you are losing money each month. Something needs to be adjusted to resolve this. You will need to figure out how to reduce the costs somehow, or increase the sales. A better idea would be to do both.

Look at the value of your profit. Is it enough to warrant going forward? Does it leave you enough to invest back into your company each month in order for it to grow?

Risk Analysis

Although you may have successfully put together a business plan that looks promising on paper, you still need to consider some other variables that could affect your business. This risk analysis thought process can help you "future-proof" your business idea. It involves thinking of all the ways that external and internal factors could hurt your business.

What are the risks of the business idea you're considering? Make a list of the potential risks that you can identify. Then, make a list of actions or processes that could reduce or mitigate those risks. This is a simple risk analysis, but it is important to perform. It is better to be prepared than to be surprised.

Some risks could be related to the business being seasonal or affected by weather conditions. Another major risk could be that of becoming obsolete due to improving technology. Your business idea may be in jeopardy if it is just based on the latest fad or trend, which could affect its longevity. Is this idea sustainable over time? Looking back at the history of economic downturns, have businesses like yours survived through depressions? Some business models even thrive in the face of chaos or destruction. It's a good exercise to think about the "what-ifs" and to plan accordingly.

How saturated is the market you are trying to enter? Does your business idea face stiff competition, with numerous other businesses offering the same products or services? Is the niche growing or declining?

Are there legal risks related to your industry or product? If so, even a company that earns a healthy profit can be wiped out by a single large lawsuit or by criminal activity.

Do you feel this risk is worth taking? Does your product infringe on any existing patented products? This should be a non-starter if you find this is the case. You may need to hire a patent attorney to do a search. It is better to pay those fees up front, rather than invest thousands of dollars and several months to discover that your product will get you sued by another company that holds the patent.

What about risks related to your location? Both brick and mortar businesses and digital businesses have location risks. Did you pick a suitable place to set up shop that will attract your ideal customers? Is there a high crime rate that could result in unexpected theft or vandalism to your property? Did you pick a location that allows you the potential to expand the size of your company if it takes off?

If your business is online, does your website hosting service do proper data backups so that you do not run the risk of losing your entire website and all your product and customer data? Does the website host have a stellar service record with minimal downtime history? If their servers go down, so does your sales revenue. Do they have the latest in website security methods to ensure hackers do not delete or alter your website? Does your website host have the capacity to quickly upgrade your server when needed, should your business website grow higher in traffic and site visits?

There are many variables to consider, but do what you can to plan how to mitigate or reduce these risks. Sometimes this simply requires more funding or more resources. Ask any business owner; we do not like surprises!

Purpose

Almost all businesses are started with a purpose in mind. Be sure to define the purpose for your business. This is usually a financial goal, as discussed earlier in this chapter, or something that involves building your legacy. Are you simply enhancing your monthly income to supplement your normal job, or are you working towards this side-hustle to transition it to become a full-time business at some point? Are you building a company to build the valuation extremely high in hopes of selling it for a windfall of cash later on? The purpose should be defined up front so that you do not waste precious time headed down the wrong financial path. Each of these goals will typically require different levels of financial and time commitment.

Scalability is a very important subject to consider. Does your business idea scale to reach the financial goals you have set? If you want to build a company with a multi-million dollar exit plan upon selling it, you have to plan for this. The strategies are much different for someone doing a side-hustle as a hobby vs. someone with larger financial goals in mind.

In our digital age, I find that online businesses offer the greatest potential for scalability. This is due to a few factors that should be considered if an exit plan to retirement is on your wants list. Online businesses open up your potential customer base to the entire world, instead of you having to rely on just customers in your immediate zip code. That is the definition of scalability! Also, if you are selling digital files as products such as e-books, audiobooks, videos, online training or services, subscription or online club memberships, software, or apps, this adds another potential layer of extreme scalability. This is because those products only require up-front development costs, and then they can be mass-produced by, essentially, copy/paste clicks of a mouse. The development cost of creating these digital products approaches zero as you sell more of them. With physical products, manufacturing costs never approach zero. Physical products also have to be shipped, which adds transportation costs. Digital products can be sent over the internet for free. They also please impulse buyers who get access to the product immediately upon paying.

Businesses based on in-person services are the most difficult to scale, as your team has to be present to perform tasks for customers. These scale in more a costly manner, such as through franchising or the building of multiple locations. Digital is just much easier to scale and at a much faster pace. Online business has created more young millionaires in this world than any other type of business.

The Exit Plan

Do you want to know the method to become a millionaire entrepreneur? The answer is simple, but the effort is not. Here is my very simple answer:

Create a systemized company that has a unique product or service and an established brand. This company needs an annual profit of at least $200,000 and a history of revenue stability or growth.

That is it. Does that sound simple to you? Well, there are also some requirements that go along with this plan. Your "unique" service cannot be based on you or any other key employee. You obviously cannot sell yourself with the company. This is where most entrepreneurs fail in terms of long-term vision. They fall into the self-employment trap and just create themselves an occupation instead of a company. The company needs to be set up as a system with defined processes and products that enable it to be managed by whoever buys the company. If you possess some unique talent or skill, you simply need to create a process to train others to do what you do. This repeatable process is what holds value to a potential buyer of your company.

Companies that do not offer unique products or services may have a harder time selling at higher values. If your business just resells items from other manufacturers, then the argument could be that your products are not unique unless you have the exclusive rights to your products. Your business model becomes less interesting to buyers if they can just create their own business and sell the exact same products themselves. You will need to have a firm grasp on the market share for generic services, have long-term contracts established, and have a backlog of work to sway buyers in your direction. They will basically be buying your contracts and backlog of work. Buyers are interested in buying the future of your company, not your past. They want to ensure there is a constant stream of inbound revenue, to be interested in purchasing your company.

If your brand name is valuable due to established reputation, market share, and partnerships in the industry, then the brand name can certainly hold extreme value on its own. This is why we say "brand matters." Brand is THE most important aspect to consider when valuation of a business happens. If your company is recognizable and popular, it is worth more to a buyer.

Valuation of your company can be handled several different ways depending on your business type. The most general valuation, as typically seen on the TV show Shark Tank, is based on the profits of your company. Technically, it is based on the EBIT, which stands for earnings before interest & taxes. For larger corporations, this acronym expands to EBITDA and includes depreciation and amortization. All of this is just a fancy acronym for saying "net profit."

The simplest valuation of a company is found by multiplying your annual net profit with a factor between 3 to 5. The more unique your brand or product is, the closer the factor approaches 5. This, essentially, means your company is worth between 3 to 5 years of your net profit. In rare circumstances, that factor may even reach much higher than 5 if your brand or products have no real market competition. This 3-5 year EBIT valuation presents a potential buyer with the opportunity to pay off their investment in 3 to 5 years. To summarize, if your company profits $200,000 per year, it could likely sell for $1M if the company is unique enough.

Before you start daydreaming, understand that not every business gets a valuation like this. If your product or service isn't unique, you have a weak branding, or your business has easy barriers of entry for starting a similar business, it could be worth much less. This may apply even if you are also profiting the same $200,000 per year.

A possible example would be a local, non-franchised auto mechanic shop. Why would someone buy your shop from you if they could literally build a shop next door to yours, buy similar equipment, and even hire your employees? In these cases, valuation of a business relies mostly on your assets owned minus liabilities (debts), plus your parts inventory at wholesale market cost. You would essentially be selling your lifts, tools, inventory, and other assets at their current depreciated market prices. Hopefully you also owned the business property and saw an increase in value over the years. This stresses the importance of establishing a stellar, recognizable brand name and producing some unique products or services.

But, don't count yourself out just yet. You can still become a millionaire with any business model as long as your profits and savings add up over enough years to total one million. Build your revenue, and increase your profits! There are many ways to get to the same goal. Not everyone wants an exit plan. Some wish to pass their company down to future generations of their family. Again, just set your own goals for the business, and tackle them in the best manner possible.

This is just a high-level understanding of corporate valuation to give you a general idea of how it works. You can search and find endless articles and books on this subject which go into greater depth. If you are ever approached to sell your business, it would be advisable to hire a professional business appraiser in order to get an estimated value of your company. You'll also want to find a business broker to represent your company during any sale activities. Be sure to find a broker that has your best interests in mind and knows your industry.

Summary Chapter 3

•   Most failed businesses tend to be started for the wrong purpose. Find something you are at least interested in doing or selling. Money follows passion.

•   Ideas are the easy part. Every single day, thousands of people die with great ideas that never get shared with the world.

•   Those not fluent in discussing business Terminology could be taken advantage of by those who are. Learn business language.

•   The best side-hustles are based on skills, knowledge or resources that you already have available.

•   Start with the end in mind. Set specific financial goals and timelines. Work backwards from these goals to define the steps necessary to achieve them.

•   Digital products that can be transferred as a file will always have the highest potential for scalability. Trading your own hours for money will have the least potential for scalability.

•   All companies should at least consider their exit plan from the beginning. You never know when you could be forced to sell your company due to factors beyond your control. Having a plan will direct many key decisions during the lifetime of the business.

Recommended Reading

•   *Start With Why* by Simon Sinek
•   *Built to Sell* by John Warrillow
•   *Blue Ocean Strategy* by Chan Kim
•   *Good to Great* by Jim Collins
•   *The E-Myth Revisited* by Michael Gerber

"All your ideas may be solid or even good... But you have to actually EXECUTE on them for them to matter."

Gary Vaynerchuk, Entrepreneur, Best-Selling Author

CHAPTER 4

BRANDING

Branding is arguably the most important aspect of your business. Branding is what creates emotions and thoughts within your customers when they hear or see your business name. It is critical that these feelings are positive, or that they resonate with your ideal customers. Think of the numerous popular brands out there; many of them do not even have to advertise their products on ads. They simply advertise their company name, knowing that they have done an amazing job at establishing their brand. You don't see Nike advertising every type of shoe they offer. Louis Vuitton doesn't create ads with their line of goods shown. Apple has placed full ads based on their vision and message rather than for any products. Other companies have even transformed the way people communicate, where their brand name has taken the place of an action. We've all heard the phrases "Please make a Xerox of this paper" and "Go and Google that." This is the power of having a good brand. Google wasn't the first search engine, but it established itself as the best.

Branding, in its most simple definition, is what people say or think about you when you are not around. This even applies to you personally, as we each have our own personal brand identity. When you approach branding like this, it makes it easier to think about how to manage your company. Do you have a clear mission that gets communicated and reaches your audience? Do you show consistency in your behaviors and actions? Are you solving people's problems with your products or service? Will your customers refer you to their friends? Have you done enough marketing to be known? These questions are all related to branding.

Create a Business Name

One of the more popular questions I receive from aspiring entrepreneurs is how to come up with a business name. I'll share my method and give you some general rules to ensure that you pick an excellent business name. Get it right the first time, as it is difficult to rebrand and have to start all over again later.

Do some brainstorming. Write down several words that you feel represent your product, service, or mission. Write down as many as possible, whatever comes to mind. Don't be afraid to be creative! You may even try combining two words to create something new. Shorter, easy to spell words are the best. You may even use online resources like Thesaurus.com to find synonyms, which are words with similar meanings. Also, think of all the businesses out there that use made up words. Google, Waze, eBay, YouTube, and Facebook are all made up words which didn't previously exist. With powerful branding, everyone knows them now. It is also important to think about your business name as your potential website address. Ideally, you'll want a website address as short in character length as possible, easy for people to remember, and something that could easily be spelled if you verbally said the website name to someone. If you can't come up with a business name that short, see if the initials of the words can form an acronym that will work. Conversely, be sure that if your business name is more than a few words that the initials aren't potentially offending. Applied Surface Specialty sounds great until you realize the acronym for it is "ASS." Also, if people can't remember your business name or website address, they won't try searching for it, either.

Rid Yourself of Fences

I typically suggest that you avoid using regional specific business names. While that worked well in the past, it doesn't serve the digital age well. In fact, having a regional name could limit your customer reach outside of the region in your name. "Houston Tires," "Nashville Shoes," or "Ohio Electronics" could create the perception that you only cater to a local market. If you want customers outside of your city and state, then avoid using those words in your business name. If you have dreams of franchising your business idea across the country, then certainly avoid regional naming. By doing this, you will avoid limiting your potential future growth due to regional bias. If you wish to serve the digital world, create a business name that is universal rather than regional.

Website Address Validation

Now that you've come up with a few ideas for business names, you must check for their availability on a domain register website. This is a fancy label for a company that will sell you the ownership rights to a custom website address, also known as the "domain name." I prefer Namecheap.com to purchase and host my website domain names. Visit their front page, and you can search available website names for free. Type in your business name idea into the "search domain" text box. You can then see if someone already owns that website address, or if you can purchase it. Try to avoid using any hyphens or underscores in any website address. For example, iconicservices.com is better than iconic-services.com, because you can't verbalize a hyphen when speaking the name to someone. It also sounds dumb when you try to speak it. "My website is iconic hyphen services dot com." Also, you only want domain names that end with .com or .net, none of the other silly ones. These are perceived to be more professional, legitimate websites. If available, buy both .com and .net variations of your name to keep someone else from cloning your site. You can make both addresses redirect to your business page later. If your full business name isn't available, see if the acronym initials are available. If the website isn't available, I'd say to move on and try some other business names. This is very important! Those made up words that were mentioned earlier are a direct result of website branding. Those companies wanted to have a short, memorable website address. You'll find that many of the names you thought you were creative are already taken. This is why some companies resort to making up words.

Don't be afraid to bounce your business name ideas off of your close network. Tell them your mission for the business, and ask their opinions on the names you have selected. You may get some interesting feedback or perceptions that you didn't consider. You may also try Google searching to see if other companies already share the same business name. This could become an issue, especially if that business exists within your same state. Since we register our businesses by state, they only allow one business per state to have a registered name. You may have to rearrange words, add words, or subtract words to make your business name unique. Or, make up a new word!

Just secure the domain name as soon as possible. We'll get into developing a website later on in this book. You really just need to purchase the domain name for now to prevent someone else from taking it.

Summary Chapter 4

•	Branding is arguably the most important aspect of your business.
•	Branding is what creates emotions and thoughts within your customers when they hear or see your business name.
•	Branding, in its most simple definition, is what people say or think about you when you are not around.
•	Branding even applies to you personally, as we each have our own personal brand identity. Do your actions represent you well?
•	Pick a website address that is short, easy to spell, and memorable.
•	Avoid using a regional word in your company name, as it could limit your expansion outside of that region.
•	If people can't remember your business name or website address, they won't try searching for it, either.

Recommended Reading

•	*Build a StoryBrand* by Donald Miller
•	*Purple Cow* by Seth Godin

"Obscurity is the single biggest killer to a business or entrepreneur."

Grant Cardone, Entrepreneur, Best-Selling Author

CHAPTER 5
MONEY

I hope that you didn't skip ahead to this chapter thinking that I somehow hid the secret to success within it. That isn't what this chapter is about. But, your grasp of the knowledge contained within this chapter will determine if your company succeeds or fails. Business finance is one giant and complex subject, a topic that could easily cover the span of numerous books. I'd encourage you to dig deeper into this topic later, but it isn't the focus of this particular book. I'll just provide some high-level thoughts to consider when starting and operating a business. I always suggest finding a good certified public accountant (CPA) to advise you and help manage your business financials. The cost of a CPA is minor compared to the business costs at risk. Ask your friends for CPA references. This topic is too important to cut corners on.

Funding

Many people stall their idea of starting a business by adopting the excuse of not having enough money to start. Rather than use this situation as a roadblock that prevents you from travelling down the road towards your dreams, let's try to reframe the idea of money. Or rather, the lack of money.

Money is simply a score. It is the score resulting from the balance of your positive vs. negative execution. This is the mindset that successful people carry. And, as with any game that keeps score, you must develop a strategy – or plays, to bring you the highest potential for scoring. Money is no different, and acquiring more of it is just a game. Lucky for us humans, our brains are wired to solve puzzles and games. There is truly no "dead end" excuse when we are discussing money. We simply have to be creative, resourceful, and put effort into making more money. That is why you picked up this book, correct? How many times has someone told you "NO" or told you something was impossible? Then you went and figured out how to do it, anyways. That is exactly how you will need to tackle the money issue if you think startup funds are lacking.

Bootstrap It

The term "bootstrap" is a funny one. It originates back to a saying from the early 19th Century in the U.S.A. It originally meant doing something impossible; to get yourself over a fence by tugging upwards on your own bootstraps. The novelty of that statement still applies to self-funding your business.

If possible, it is always better to fund your own business 100% on your own. This means you will not have any loans to repay, which would eat into your monthly profits. It means you will not have any partners to split your profits with. Thinking further down the road, it could mean you won't have others to split the millions received in an exit plan. I find that many people partner up unnecessarily. They seem to do this in order to share some of the financial risk, or to feel they aren't alone in the effort. It tends to be more of the latter, a mental security blanket. But, the financial impact is huge! If you are going to start your business by cutting your pie into many other pieces, then hopefully all of your partners have decided the target revenue will be able to provide the desired lifestyle for each of you. You don't always need partners. You can later hire consultants and employees to handle tasks that you aren't good at. Fund the business yourself, and you will receive all the rewards yourself.

How do you "bootstrap" fund your own business? By figuring out how to earn and save more money. There are numerous ways you can do this.

- Sell the stuff you don't need.
- Work extra hours at your current job if available.
- Pick up a 2nd or 3rd part-time job.
- Reduce your monthly bills and expenses to save more.
- Downsize your current lifestyle.

Staircase Businesses

Sometimes people are only focused on starting their perfect, dream business. Sometimes that dream business isn't financially realistic at this time. So, this is when you should begin thinking of starting smaller with what I call "staircase businesses." Think of businesses that you can start immediately based on your current skills, talents, knowledge, or resources. These businesses can provide extra income that could be put towards your dream business. Your dream business could simply be a few staircase businesses away from happening. If you want to start that $10M dream business, maybe you need to build up a few $1M companies first to create that investment size. In baseball, we don't always swing for the homerun at each at-bat. Sometimes we have to think in terms of strategy, and hit an infield single or bunt. Don't rule out starting small for now to work towards large later. Sitting around and claiming you can't start because you can't afford your dream business is unproductive. Complaining doesn't move you closer to your goal. Figuring out another path does.

Get a Loan

While it has become increasingly difficult to get small business loans in recent years, there are still banks out there that are willing to fund well-planned businesses. You may even qualify for a government-backed SBA loan, which is an acronym for Small Business Association. You can find details about these loans on the federal website www.sba.gov if you are interested. Do some searching, and you'll find various ways to get loans if your credit is good and your business plan is solid.

Another popular way for people to fund their companies is to take out a home equity loan. If you have a positive equity in your mortgage, you can usually borrow up to 80% of that equity value.

Another form of loan is more readily available, and it lives in your wallet. Credit cards. Thousands of successful small businesses have been started by working off of credit cards. But, keep in mind that these loans are also very high interest, especially if you do not pay off the balance each month. You may have to continually flip your balance from one card to another in order to take advantage of introductory periods with reduced interest rates. This can be a hassle, and you'll need to manage it, but the opportunity exists.

What about a personal loan from family or friends? Got any stragglers out there that still owe you money? It is past time you collect on that nonsense. If your dream is important to you, find the courage to ask. You may be surprised at who offers to help.

Crowdfunding

This has recently become a more popular way of raising capital for startups and inventions. You essentially have to put together a good business plan, and pitch it online at one of the various crowdfunding websites. If your story and product are compelling and interesting enough, you may have hundreds or thousands of people donate to be a part of your journey. The added benefit of this method is that you also gain a lot of cheerleaders who have a vested interest in seeing your business succeed. They almost become a social media marketing team for you, as they share your idea with their networks. There are several websites for this, such as Kickstarter.com, GoFundMe.com, and IndieGoGo.com, each of which has helped create some amazing brands. Go study how other brands have pitched their companies, and take notes from the popular examples.

Banking

It is important to create an entirely new bank account to handle your business. This will make it much easier for you to monitor and track expenses and income received from business. This is really important when it comes tax time! It would be utter chaos to have to dig back through your own personal banking statements to comb out all of the business related expenses and income. Get yourself a business checking account and a debit/credit card, as well as business checks. Ideally, you will want this account to be created under your business name. This could be as a DBA (doing business as), LLC, S corporation, however you end up registering your business. We'll discuss the differences of those later. If you do not register the account using a company name, you will have to use your own social security number to register it. When you register an account using a company, you use the company EIN number instead. This stands for employer identification number, and every registered company receives their own unique number. Think of it as the federal social security number for your company. You will also file your business taxes with the EIN number.

Get Paid

The objective of a business is to get paid, right? That means you need to establish at least one account to accept payments from customers. There are a few online banking accounts that allow this; your business checking account may even have a service that provides this. If not, then you'll need to set up another account with another company that handles payments. This way you'll be able to receive payments from credit cards, wire transfers, and even online checks. One thing to understand is that these payment accounts all earn money from transaction fees. Generally, they want 2-3% of every transaction that passes through them. This is what most major credit cards charge in order for you to be able to accept credit cards as payment. You cannot avoid this, but there are ways to help combat this percentage. You might consider using a cash-back type rewards program card to make business purchases or pay business bills. That typically earns you back at least 1-2% credit on the purchases you make for your business.

I've used PayPal.com for over 18 years now to process my credit card payments. I find it very simple to use, and it's easy for my customers to use. PayPal basically uses your email address as your bank account number. This means anyone with an email address essentially has a possible bank account number with PayPal. I've literally moved multiple millions through PayPal without a hassle. I just transfer any funds received from my PayPal account over to my bank checking account each week. This is all done online very easily. I also like that I can download all of my sales and purchase history reports from them to use for filing quarterly taxes. There are several online banking companies that offer similar services; you'll just need to browse them to find which one works for you. Popular choices include Stripe, Google Wallet, and several others. Most even have cell phone apps that allow you to receive payments in person by typing in the credit card digits. Some may even have an attachment that plugs into your cell phone to swipe credit cards. Pay attention to the fees that each company charges for the type of transactions that you plan on doing most. Always read the fine print. You may find that one brand of payment service is better for you when compared to the others.

Cash Flow

Money is the lifeblood of your business. Think of this in a literal sense, as money works about the same way as blood in your body. You must have enough blood flowing through your body to transport oxygen to all its areas. Your business will also require enough money to operate properly in all its areas. This really depends on your business model, as some require more money than others to operate. This is the importance of cash flow. Mismanaged businesses often starve themselves to death due to cash flow by not understanding how this process works.

You will need money to purchase inventory products or raw goods for manufacturing. You will need money to pay employees and hire external services. With most businesses, you can't sell what you don't have. Your goal here is always to remain "cash positive," which means you have enough money to spend to operate the business while you wait on customers to buy something from you. Being "cash negative" means you do not have enough money, and it is hurting your day-to-day operations, slowing progress, and limiting your potential.

You will have to calculate how much money your company requires to keep operating properly. Always carry extra in the account. You never know when there will be a downturn in your business. What if a product shipment arrives late, and you don't get paid when you thought you would? You never know when you will have a customer that refuses to pay you or is very slow to pay you back. If you don't have enough money, a simple incident could put you out of business. Most cash flow bankruptcies often happen like a series of dominoes falling down, and they are triggered by an initial incident. You will go out of business when you owe more than you can pay.

When working with customers on a longer contract basis, or when performing a longer period of service for them, be sure to structure the payments to you so that you remain cash positive at all phases of the project. We call these milestone payments. These multiple milestone payments are percentages of the total contract value, but they are paid to you as you complete each major task. An example for a home remodel service would be to charge the customer for the parts, and then get the parts ordered. Then charges would occur again when each critical task of labor has been performed. Bathroom complete? Charge for that. Kitchen complete? Charge for that. This keeps your financial risk low should any disagreement arise during the course of the project. Always strive to be cash positive on deals when possible. This will give you a little leverage if the deal goes sour. At the very least, aim for being cash neutral. This means both the buyer and the seller share the same financial risk in the transaction. If you define milestone payments properly, this can be achieved. Cash neutral means the customer isn't overpaying at any time, and you aren't underpaid at any time. Always get these long-term agreements in writing! As any lawyer will tell you, "If it isn't in writing, it doesn't exist." Too many small businesses have been shut down by being too trusting, just like too many customers have been scammed for also being too trusting. Protect yourself. It is your duty as a business owner. Don't be willing to risk not getting paid if you know it could kill your company.

Return On Investment (ROI)

If you've ever heard the phrase "It takes money to make money," then you've been introduced to ROI. You've likely heard "ROI" if you work within any corporate setting. Get used to this acronym when you run a business. ROI is linked to cash flow, and once you think in this mindset, you will begin to scrutinize every single expense that occurs within your company. This has nothing to do with saving money! So many small business owners think too small, and they're always trying to save a buck. Money is meant to be invested to create growth. It isn't meant to be saved away in some low-interest bank account. Why earn 3% per year in a savings account, when that same money could earn you much more if you invested it into your company properly?

Think in terms of "return on investment." For every dollar spent, what is the financial return? If you handed me $100 and I gave you back $200, that would be an excellent return. Who wouldn't do that? If you could spend $10,000 on advertising and receive $20,000 in profit from the sales generated by the ad, wouldn't that $10,000 be worth spending? Absolutely. It doubled your money. This is the proper mindset for a business owner. Do not be afraid to spend what it takes to earn more or grow more. Monitor every expense you pay for, and understand what the financial benefit for that expense is.

This mindset will also keep you from spending money on stupid stuff that adds no value or profit to your company. It will make you identify areas of your company where there is more profit, and you should begin to spend any extra dollars in that area instead. You can apply ROI to anything in a company. Building location and cost, marketing, employee salaries, external services, anything that has a cost. Do the costs justify themselves with a financial return? If so, you are on a good path. Delete or reduce anything that costs you more than the value it brings in. Or, find better ROI alternatives.

Taxes

Now that you've hopefully made all this money, you can count on the state and federal government to want their share of it. This process has gotten much easier in the last few years, as most tax entities have moved to online reporting and payments.

State taxes will vary within each state. Some require quarterly sales tax filings, and some have annual filings. You will need to know your sales tax laws for the state you operate in. At the time of this writing, you only have to collect state sales tax from customers who purchase from within the same state as your business. If you own businesses in multiple states, you will also have to collect sales tax from customers in each of those states. Be sure to put this tax money aside, and keep track of how much within your bank account will go towards state taxes. You'll have to pay that amount to the state when you file each time. Also, some states have income taxes, and those will be filed separately from sales taxes. Again, this reporting period and filing method will vary by state.

Federal income tax is filed annually with the IRS. If your business is very complex, this could be a chore. If it is something you are not interested in doing, there are plenty of certified public accountants out there who are ready and willing to help. Throughout the business year, just be sure to keep all expense and business purchase receipts, transaction reports, sales reports, state taxes paid, losses, and anything related to financials. Your accountant will need all this info at the end of the year. Get into a good habit of just saving this stuff as you go, rather than scrambling at the end of the year to locate all this stuff. There are also many choices of software and apps out there which can make it easy for you to track financials for your business. Check out their reviews online, ask around, and select one that works best for you.

Summary Chapter 5

•   Your grasp of financial management will determine if your business succeeds or fails.

•   Think of money as just a score. It is the score resulting from the balance of your positive vs. negative execution.

•   Always have a separate bank account for your business, so that there is a clear split from your personal financials.

•   Mismanaged businesses often starve themselves to death due to cash flow issues.

•   Money is meant to be re-invested to create growth. It isn't meant to be saved away in some low-interest bank savings account.

•   Keep all business records. All of them. If there is a $ symbol shown within a document, save a copy. Your CPA will want these to perform your tax services.

Recommended Reading

•   *Profit First* by Mike Michalowicz
•   *Rich Dad's Cashflow Quadrant* by Robert Kiyosaki

"It's not how much money you make, but how much money you keep, how hard it works for you, and how many generations you keep it for."

Robert Kiyosaki, Entrepreneur, Best-Selling Author

CHAPTER 6

STRUCTURE

One question that always gets asked is "What type of business structure do I need?" To someone just getting started, the information available can be overwhelming to sort through. I'll try my best to simplify the differences between a DBA, LLC, and a corporation. My hope here is that you'll gain a high-level understanding of each. This should help shorten your learning curve so that you can start focusing and learning about the specific one that best suits your business type.

The main reason we use company structures is to create a defined line between the owner(s) and the company. This is primarily for tax reporting and accounting purposes. The other reason is to provide protection for the owner(s) in case of potential events such as bankruptcy, loan defaults, or lawsuits.

In most states, you do not need to have a company name if you simply use your own name as the business. This is what is known as a "sole proprietorship" business. This means there is only one owner/employee, and you are self-employed. Any income the sole proprietorship receives goes directly to you. There is no defined line between the owner and the business. But, there are risks to be aware of, as mentioned previously.

If you do not want to use your personal name as the business name, the simplest business to create is the DBA, which stands for "doing business as." This is basically an alias name you choose to do business under. The DBA company name can be an alias for an individual or even another company. The DBA exists purely to provide transparency, so that customers can understand who the actual person or company is that they are doing business with. The DBA will still use your personal social security number to track the financials and registration. It is no different than a sole proprietorship in function. It just defines a business name being used.

Generally, creating a DBA just requires filling out a registration form within your local county or state. This is usually done through the Secretary of State office of the state you reside in or the state you wish to register the company in. Most of this process has been moved to online registration nowadays. The DBA is inexpensive to create. It usually has a small registration fee and a small renewal fee. Renewals average about five years, depending on the state.

Although the DBA setup is inexpensive and simple, there is one major negative of operating solely with just a DBA. The DBA offers you no protection from lawsuits. If someone decides to sue your DBA company, they can actually go after your personal assets. If you registered a DBA through one of your registered companies, they can sue the parent company. All liability is taken by whoever owns the DBA. You simply need to define the potential risks of the products or services you offer, and the likelihood that someone could sue because of either. There are millions of DBAs out there operating just fine, but you should just be aware of the risks associated with your type of business. Only you can determine if you need an added layer of protection.

The limited liability corporation (LLC) is the most commonly used entity for small businesses. As the name implies, you gain legal protection as your liability is now limited. If someone sues your LLC, they can only go after the assets of the company – not your personal assets. This is because the LLC is actually a separate entity. The LLC will not use your social security number like the DBA does; it will have a federally issued employee identification number (EIN) that is used for financial tracking and reporting. The LLC is registered through the state you reside in, or the state that you wish to set up the company within. There are more forms to fill out, which have to be distributed to state and federal offices. Most of this process can be streamlined by online companies such as LegalZoom.com, who perform the background work for you, for a single fee.

The LLC is often the best choice if you are a small company that plans on having few employees. Generally, the LLC is ideal for smaller, privately-owned companies that do not have stocks or shareholders. It offers most of the protections of larger corporations, but less of the burdensome process and report filing requirements.

Because the LLC is a separate entity from the owner(s), it will require yearly IRS tax filing. Most states also require you to file quarterly sales tax filings, which report your total sales and in-state sales separately. During these quarterly sales tax filings, you will pay your state the sales tax that you've collected from selling products or services within your same state.

The C corporation is another business structure that best suits a larger company that is targeted for growth. This structure requires more formal documentation and process than an LLC, such as requiring a formal structure of shareholders, directors, officers, and employees. Also, the corporation is required to appoint at least one person to serve on the board of directors, and the officers are required to oversee the day-to-day operations of the business. If this sounds too complicated for your business model, it likely is. The tax filing is also more complicated than the LLC, which is also a deterrent for small business owners.

There is also another business structure called an S corporation, which has a unique tax filing format where all profits are passed down through the owners (shareholders) and are processed as their personal income. The S corporation does not do individual tax filing as an entity.

There are complete books written on each of these business structures, but hopefully you've gained conversational insight on the differences of each. I'd recommend you contact a trusted tax attorney or business advisor if you require more stringent details. There are also numerous resources online to teach you the differences. I've found that LLCs tend to be the most common for small business owners due to the ease of tax filing and the layer of legal protection offered.

If your business type will be purchasing and reselling goods or services, you will need a sales and use tax permit. This is a permit that you register for through your state office, which allows you to avoid paying sales tax on items that you intend to resell. Your suppliers will ask for a copy of this permit for their records, as they have to report these transactions for their business tax filing.

Currently, you are only obligated to charge for and collect state sales tax from customers who purchase from the same state your company exists within. If you are selling items across state lines, there is no sales tax collected. As mentioned previously, this collected state sales tax gets paid to your state on a quarterly basis during quarterly sales tax filing.

Summary Chapter 6

• The main reason we use company structures is to create a defined line between the owner(s) and the company.

• This separation will provide protection for the owner(s) in case of potential events such as bankruptcy, loan defaults, or lawsuits.

• Operating under a DBA offers a business owner no protection. It is only to provide transparency to customers about who they are actually doing business with.

• The LLC tends to be the most commonly used business structure for small businesses. It offers protection, and it minimizes paperwork and process.

• The corporation structures are best suited for companies that will have several employees, executives, and shareholders.

"The bottom line is that you are the one who is creating your life the way it is. The life you currently live is the result of all your past thoughts and actions. You are in charge of your current thoughts and your present feelings."

Jack Canfield, Entrepreneur, Best-Selling Author

CHAPTER 7
MARKETING

There is a popular saying that you've likely heard: "It isn't what you know, it is who you know." I prefer a variation of this phrase, as it applies to business. My version states: "It isn't who you know, it is who knows you." This is your presence or omnipresence. It is your skill at being on other people's minds, or on the tips of their tongues – for good reasons, hopefully. Think of it this way; you could be the very best person in the world at doing something, but it will not matter if people don't know you or where to find you. Welcome to modern marketing.

Tell a Story

In the current digital age, we are flooded daily by images, videos, music, celebrity spokespeople, and numerous other forms of advertising. Too many companies focus too much on putting their product in front of your eyes. They focus too much on selling something to you, rather than telling you a story.

Humans are fascinated by stories, and we tend to buy based on emotion. We have grown numb to generic product sales ads. We want to be given value by companies before we open our wallets to them. We want to know their backstory, and find it relatable. The story should inspire, educate, or entertain us. The story should describe a pain point or problem that we have, and then tell us how the company will solve this problem for us. It may be a popular story of overcoming adversity or personal challenge to inspire us. A story that welcomes us into a group, where a product makes us feel like a part of a movement or something bigger than ourselves.

These story methods are time-tested, brilliant methods of marketing. Yet, so many companies just fail at this process. They think they should continue to stick a product in your face, and tell you a price. That is not interesting. This even trickles down to the small business owners on their social media accounts. Nobody likes to follow someone that just posts stuff for sale all the time. If I get a friend request on Facebook, and their entire profile page is just a bunch of selling stuff or services…delete. That would be like inviting more junk mail into your mailbox outside. Business owners should certainly use their personal profiles to help market their business, but they need to do this with better strategy and tactics.

Here is a better way of marketing via your social media profile. First, you need to cleanse your page. You should always view your profile page from the perspective of a new visitor. Someone who doesn't know you. Basically, a potential customer's perspective. If you were looking at your own profile page as a current or potential customer, what would turn you off? Are you posting extremely biased topics that may polarize customers? Are you sharing immature videos and memes or goofy Snapchat dog-face photos of yourself? Are you doing anything that does not enhance your company branding? If so, hit the delete button. Numerous times, if necessary. Curious customers will scroll several pages down your feed to see what you are all about. Now, you may be thinking with your ego at this moment. You might be saying: "You know what? Screw those people! I am who I am! They shouldn't judge." But, this line of thinking doesn't help with reality. You are certainly judged by numerous things, no matter how much society likes to float out the feel-good statements that promote not being judged. Basic human nature doesn't listen to memes or philosophical jargon. You will be judged whether you accept it or not. If you are serious about promoting your company, and your business is a priority, then you must act accordingly to promote it. Doing so will absolutely affect your bottom line.

Now that you've combed the bugs out of your profile page, you must adopt a mindset that carefully curates what you post from now on. With each post you make, you have to ask yourself one simple question: "Does this post help, or potentially hurt my brand?" It really is just a yes or no question. If the answer isn't an absolutely positive "yes," then assume it's a negative idea to share something. The most important thing is to avoid just always posting about your products or services. You'll get unfollowed in a hurry if you are always asking people to open their wallet. This is the exact opposite reaction that we want if we are marketing online. We want more attention! Attention can be considered a currency. Just like with money, you want to attract more positive attention and make it grow. The more people that follow, watch and observe you, the higher odds you have of gaining potential customers. Share interesting things that you feel your ideal customers would enjoy. Show people that you are human, especially if you lead an interesting life. Entertain people with amusing stories of your own. Share your vulnerabilities so that people will relate to your story. If you have some advice that could help people, share it without asking for anything in return. The goal here is to provide far more value, more often, before asking for anything. I recommend that you only ask for something in 1 out of 10 posts. This will keep people from unfollowing you, and new visitors to your profile page will not immediately think you are just some spammer that only posts stuff for sale. They will accept your friend requests. They will think of you when the time to purchase comes. They will share your stories, resulting in free advertising exposure.

Marketing Strategy

While it may seem intuitive to want to showcase how versatile your company is with all the talents that you have…marketing does not work well in this manner. You must take on a smaller niche with a more precise focus – especially when just getting started. Think of this as being similar to when someone has a specific disease that requires treatment. They do not seek out a general practice doctor; they seek out a specialist. They want someone with very specific expertise to help solve their problem. Marketing is exactly like this. You must reduce your broad marketing ideas and focus to solve one problem. This could be done for your entire business model or each specific product, but the marketing must be precise and follow a target niche.

Any business exists to solve problems for customers. The customer's "problem" might just be boredom and wanting to be entertained. Perhaps their problem is not having a vacation planned. It could be simply a perceived lack of status, so they want some luxury brand item or upscale vehicle. Maybe the problem is a task or chore that they would like to accomplish easier. Each product or service simply solves a unique problem. The better that you can describe a problem that customers relate to, and the better you can convince them that you have the solution, the more likely they will make a purchase. There are billions of people out there, and no shortage of customers. If you aim too broadly and try to market solving numerous problems, you become a generalist. Not an expert. Experts always earn more than generalists. Remember this.

Once your company is more established, you can always expand it to increase product lines or services. But for now, stay focused on your core business and your ideal customer. Create marketing that entertains, inspires, educates and attracts that perfect customer. What is a perfect customer? As a business owner, you likely have in mind who the perfect customer is. Take a moment to write down the characteristics and demographics of this person, so that you can customize your marketing to specifically attract them. List their age range, sex, location, financial status, hobbies or interests, companies or brands they might follow or use, and other factors that make them the ideal customer. Your marketing needs to speak directly to them, define a specific problem they have, and say how you will solve it.

Currently, Facebook advertising is still the best value for the dollar spent. At any given time, the app of popularity may change. Remember all of those demographics you just wrote down for your ideal customer? You can select that criteria when advertising on Facebook to ensure that your ad is placed directly in front of ideal customers. You won't be wasting precious ad money on putting the ad in front of the wrong people. This is very powerful advertising. There are entire books on this strategy, but my goal here is just to inform you enough that you know this potential exists. That is just scratching the surface, really. With powerful ads that utilize "Facebook Pixel" or "Google Pixel," you can track visitors to your website, and track their habits and other pages they frequent. Then you can purchase targeted ads from Facebook or Google using those criteria to hone in on perfect customers. That is the reason why you will always see the ads for products show up on your Facebook feed from other websites you recently browsed. They tracked your visit, and the advertisers paid to follow you around the internet. With voice technology quickly on the rise via Apple's Siri and Google's Alexa, you can be certain that those technologies will eventually be listening to your conversations for keywords or brand names…and strategically placing ads on your screen the next time you fire it up. The marketing world is very tech-savvy and proactive nowadays. It isn't simply putting up billboards and buying some magazine page space. Those passive forms of advertising are all but dead.

Consistency

Marketing consistency is a subject that you may not see being discussed in other marketing or startup based books. I feel it is important enough to bring up, as I've seen so many businesses start extremely strong with marketing and then taper off into oblivion. Sometimes they never recover, and many go out of business because of this lack of consistency.

I see so many companies doing things poorly. These companies act as if marketing isn't a priority or worth putting a real effort behind. This has always confused me, as I know that excellent marketing can absolutely launch a company from out of nowhere. We've all witnessed this. Think of some unknown company that caught your eye with unique and extraordinary marketing, which made you curious enough to look them up. That is the power of good marketing. Even when we know the power of good marketing, how come we still have companies failing at it?

The companies that lose momentum have just had no directive to maintain consistency. They became complacent. Whoever was in charge of their marketing simply failed at seeing the big picture. These companies feel that marketing is just used for attracting enough customers to fill the capacity of sales that the company can produce. When they start to get busy or get behind in orders, they slack on their marketing effort. I've literally had clients say, "We're too busy, already. I don't need more marketing." This is a terrible mindset which should be corrected.

Customers appreciate when your company maintains a consistent behavior in marketing. This shows that your company is dependable and values being known. It shows that your company is relevant and still around. Even if your company is extremely busy, realize that this may just be a temporary state. The customers that are waiting on products or service know you are still around, because they are engaged in a transactional deal with you at the moment. But, when you quit advertising, nobody else knows you still exist. You aren't feeding the pipeline for future customers to think of you. Haven't you ever asked yourself if some company was "still around" or "still in business"? While that company could be bursting at the seams with business, they are exhibiting poor marketing strategy. The best of the best companies will keep that throttle floored, maintain market share, and keep showing omnipresence even when they are at capacity. Omnipresence is being in more than one place at all times. Your goal is to become the first brand someone thinks of whenever they have a need for a product or service you offer, or the first they think of if someone else asks them for a referral. This is how your business remains relevant, and nobody ever wonders if you are "still around."

In business, competition never rests. You must run your business like someone is always trying to put you out of business, because essentially – your competitors are. You must climb and claw your way to the top of your market niche, and never be willing to relinquish that position. You can't keep the throne by becoming complacent, especially when it comes to marketing.

Summary Chapter 7

- It isn't about who you know, it is about who knows you.
- Businesses focus too much on selling something to us, rather than telling us a story. The story is what attracts. Appeal to emotions, not logic.
- You will be judged by numerous things, no matter how much society likes to float out the feel-good statements that promote not being judged.
- Your business must take on a smaller niche with more precise focus – especially when just getting started.
- Any business exists simply to solve problems for customers.
- Too many businesses start extremely strong with marketing, and then taper off into oblivion. Sometimes they never recover, and many go out of business because of this lack of consistency.
- You goal is to become the first brand someone thinks of whenever they have a need for a product or service you offer or if someone else asks them for a referral.
- You can't keep the throne by becoming complacent, especially when it comes to marketing.

Recommended Reading

- *How to Win Friends and Influence People in The Digital Age* by Dale Carnegie
- *Jab, Jab, Jab, Right Hook* by Gary Vaynerchuk
- *Attractive Story Selling* by Mike Fallat
- *Shoe Dog* by Phil Knight

"Dream so big everyone thinks you're crazy, no matter what they think about it. The only person that limits you stares back at you in the mirror every single day."

Andy Frisella, Entrepreneur, Podcaster, Author

CHAPTER 8
WEBSITE

Now that you've got your branding and marketing strategies in place, it is time to build your digital hub of activity. Having a website is a highly critical element for nearly every business model. Think of your website as the first impression that the majority of your customers will experience about your company. What do you want your opening impression to tell them? If you put up an unprofessional, sloppy, low-budget looking website…what will that tell customers about your quality or level of service? They may begin to wonder what other aspects of your business that you cut corners on or have no care about. I recommend that you do the website development once, and do it right the first time. Once the website is set up, most require little to no maintenance going forward.

Setting up a website is much easier nowadays than any time before. Even if you've never had any experience building a website, there are numerous do-it-yourself (DIY) website hosting companies and online apps available to help make the process somewhat simple. You really only have two options to get a website up and running. Either pay someone else to do it – or be adventurous and learn something on your own. If you can type words on a keyboard and drag images around on a Word document or slideshow presentation, then you likely have enough skill to build a nice website.

Logo Design

You've established your business name, but you need a nice logo to represent your company. This is important for branding! Think about it. The best companies you can think of all have some sort of easily identifiable logo. Their logo may not even contain any words, and you can spot them from a distance and know what brand they are. That is the power of good branding. It is simply about recognition. You want to have an icon that customers will identify with instantly.

Unless you are savvy with Photoshop, Illustrator, or some other digital graphics software, I'd suggest you keep this simple. There are a few freelancer based websites available filled with designers on standby waiting for your project. A very popular website for all sorts of freelance work is Fiverr.com. When you visit this site, you can type in a search for the type of work you need performed. You will find logo designers out there that will work for as little as $5! Fiverr has freelancers located all around the world, and the strength of your local currency relative to theirs can make this a win-win for both buyer and creator. Simply type in "logo design" in the search feature, and you'll find hundreds of designers with different styles and methods available. You can view their profile to see their feedback ratings from previous customers. You can compare their skills. You will see the various packages they offer, and prices for each. I suggest you "hire" two or three designers for your logo, since they are inexpensive. Then, in a couple days, you'll have several to choose from. Make this a fun event with your friends and family. Have them help pick out the best logo. As someone just getting started, you may find all sorts of business related services from freelancers on sites like Fiverr.

Design Strategy

Before we get into building and designing your website, I feel it is important to discuss some design strategy and philosophy for websites. I see far too many websites done poorly, and I want to make sure that yours is done well.

The most important visual part of any website is the main page, specifically the area known as "above the fold." This is the section that you immediately see when you first arrive on a website that fills the screen before you ever scroll downwards. It is critical that this above the fold section contains just enough information to convey what your company does. A visitor should never arrive on any website and wonder to themselves, "What does this company do? What do they sell?" This section of your website should answer that question for them in order to immediately grab their attention. This section should be relatively simple, clean, and not too distracting with busy graphics or a bunch of links and text everywhere. It just needs to serve to (1) identify your brand, and (2) tell people what you do.

The description of your company does not require a lengthy paragraph explaining all the services or products you sell. On the contrary, actually. Too much information in this section is actually distracting and not recommended. Most well-designed websites often contain the brand logo near the top of the screen, a simple background image that relates to the company products or services, and one simple sentence that tells a visitor what you do. Think of this sentence as your most simplified "elevator pitch" or mission statement. If you had to describe your business in one simple sentence, what would you say? Here are some examples:

For a T-shirt retailer:
"Custom made shirts that tell your story."
Marketing agency:
"We ensure your potential customers find you."
Real estate group:
"Let us help find your dream home, today."
Automotive performance shop:
"We will make your fast car go even faster."
Coaching:
"Gain confidence and knowledge to reach higher levels."

In each of these examples, you may notice a trend. The statements are presented in such a way that they are helping to solve a problem for a potential customer. Your website is never supposed to be about talking all about your company! This is especially true on the main page. The "about us" page of your website is where you should list out the company history, merits, experience, and other information about your company. People generally do not care about the details of your company. They only care about what problem you can solve for them. A poorly designed main page consists of too much detail about the company itself, as if you are really just marketing the company to others. If they are on your website, you already did enough marketing to get them there, somehow. Now that you have their attention, you need to focus on solving their pain point. What problem do they have that you can help them with? This mindset shift to the customer's perspective is very important, and it should guide your entire design process for your website. Your entire main page should be devoted to representing your company as merely a knowledgeable guide, which only serves to help people solve their problems.

Another good thing to have on your main page are customer testimonials. Bonus points if these are on video! Video testimonials have historically had the highest conversion rate of turning browsing customers into purchasers. Numerous studies about consumer psychology show that most people never like to feel they are the first to buy something, so they inherently trust the testimonials of others to make a decision. Most website designers suggest having at least three customer testimonials presented, but no more than six. This would be further down the page, not something in the above the fold section.

These design subjects offer just a taste of website design strategy. There are numerous experts and books that focus on this subject. But, with the basic ideas presented above, you'll be off to a great start. You should have already purchased your website address (aka domain name), and there are simple steps to follow with website hosts in order to use your website address for your new website.

DIY Website

For those of you willing to give it a shot and build your own website, there are several website hosts and software formats available. The most simple would be one of the various DIY, build-it-yourself website companies which also offer hosting for your website. Think of the host as some location on the internet where your website is parked and made accessible at all times. You will be able to edit and update your website from the host's control panel screen once you have an account with them. You will be able to practice, learn, and completely design and build a website privately. Visitors to your website only get to see the site once it is published. Even when it is published, you can continue to make revisions and updates in the background, and then just publish the newest version.

To find a website host company, use Google to search "DIY website builder," and you will find several companies to choose from. These searches will also find articles that rate the quality, support, and service from these companies. All reviews are worth reading. Some popular DIY sites are Wix, Weebly, 1and1, and Squarespace. You may find that just because some host company names are more popular, it doesn't necessarily mean they are better. It just means those popular brands spend more on advertising, and they have built up name recognition. Pick a company, and sign up for a hosted website package using their online website building software.

With most of these DIY website builders, you can typically browse the company's online catalog of website templates or themes as a starting point. These themes will be the visual layout of your page. Don't worry about feeling locked into your first decision, as most hosts allow you to change themes at any time. Find a theme that resonates with your company that you feel will attract ideal customers best.

Once you have the theme selected, you simply work around the page and add content on the page. Attach photos, create text, add graphics, videos and such. This usually involves uploading those files from your computer onto the host's server, and then selecting them from a file once they are uploaded onto the host. Most can be dragged to location with a mouse, resized, and such. This is really simple stuff! You can also create new pages that link from your main website page. These new pages are typically things like about us, contact, products, services and other suitable things that you feel require their own page.

Wordpress Website

For a more customizable website, most companies are now moving to Wordpress online software to create their sites. Wordpress is a bit more complicated to set up than the DIY formats presented above, but it offers far more custom features and add-ons (called "plug-ins"). You can either use a reduced version hosted at Wordpress.com, or a more deluxe version using Wordpress.org. Your Wordpress based website will also require a website host, and many website hosts offer Wordpress packages that neatly include the software that allow you to create and edit your page. These package deals also make things convenient, as the host will install the Wordpress software and set up the server structure for you. Once your account is set up with a host, you will build your website using the admin panel online. Like the DIY type sites, Wordpress offers thousands of potential themes to start from. Some are free, and many of them cost a little bit for a 1-time purchase license. I've seen a typical range from $20 to $100 for a license to use one of the premium themes. Wordpress gets the advantage of having numerous other companies, developers, and designers that use this software format to create plug-ins, themes, tools, and offerings that will enhance or automate functions on your page. You can seamlessly integrate your social media updates to your page, create beautiful blog posts and articles, and essentially control every visual aspect of your page. While DIY pages can certainly look great, a Wordpress page can be customized to take it to another level. If you need help setting up a Wordpress page or theme, you can also find freelancers that have these skills over at the previously mentioned Fiverr.com. Sometimes it is just best to pay an expert, rather than waste weeks learning. The site can then be relatively simple for you to edit or update once the theme styling and graphics are set up and functioning.

For new business owners with limited website building experience, I'd still recommend one of the DIY websites as their first website. Their ease of use, low cost, and simplicity are great for any startup business. If the business grows in revenue and profit, then you may justify a website upgrade later on. Keep it simple and functional! Remember to design your website from a customer's perspective, not your company's perspective.

Custom Email Account

Some website hosts will offer to provide you with one of their own email inboxes using your website domain address. I do not recommend using these email accounts. One main reason is that many of these companies make it very difficult for you to transfer your emails and contacts out, should you decide to move to a different host later. That means you could lose months or even years of emails and data later on. That is never good! Another reason is that these free accounts are difficult to customize, organize, and log into. They are really clunky and inefficient in most cases.

Instead of using the free email accounts, create a new Google Gmail "G Suite" business account. Visit gsuite.google.com, and then select either the $5 or $10 per month package based on your needs. Follow their instructions on how to create a business email account that uses your website domain address. This makes your business look more professional by having @businessname.com as your email address. It looks very sloppy when someone uses a generic email address for their business, such as @yahoo.com, @gmail.com, @aol.com, etc. It is very simple to create this Gmail G Suite account with all of Google's functionality and your custom email address. You also get the added benefit of the other Google business support apps, such as their integrated calendar. This calendar works great for setting appointments, meetings, events, vacation days and having reminders reach you via email or text notifications.

Summary Chapter 8

•	Think of your website as the first impression of your company that the majority of your customers will experience.
•	The most important visual part of any website is the main page, specifically the area known as "above the fold." This is the first thing you see before scrolling down.
•	If you had to describe your business in one simple sentence, what would you say?
•	Customers generally do not care about the details of your company. They only care about what problem you can solve for them.
•	Using a custom email address with your own website domain looks more professional to customers.

"It's not about making it perfect, it's about taking action, getting a result, and adjusting accordingly."

Mel Robbins, Best-Selling Author

CHAPTER 9

CONCLUSION

If you've made it to this point in the book, I applaud you. Statistics say that most books go unfinished. This is either a statement of how awfully most books are written, or an illustration of how most people are just not that committed. I'm going to take the latter reason. You have proven that you are truly dedicated to building something.

To fully capture every bit of knowledge and nuance of creating and operating a business, it would take what more closely resembles a volume of encyclopedias. Remember those? That was never the purpose of this book. My intention is to get you up to speed quickly and to shorten your learning curve. Having completed this book, you are now armed with enough knowledge and resources to actually start your business. You should now have much more confidence during conversations around the topics discussed.

While you now should be capable of navigating the process of starting a business, you are never done learning. Entire books exist on the subjects presented within each chapter of this book. There are paid professionals that specialize in each specific chapter as well. Whenever you feel you need to strengthen in a specific area, I urge you to learn more about that subject. Even as a successful entrepreneur, I've continued to learn almost daily for my entire life. Sometimes lessons are right before our eyes, but we are too blind to see them. Never be afraid of learning as you go.

Starting is the most important thing you can do. There will never be that perfect time, as that time is now.

CHAPTER 10
JOURNEY

Here I sit at my desk, writing the last chapter of my first book. Truth be told, I've had this book inside me for several years. I just kept putting off writing it. What stories or businesses are you keeping bottled up inside of you? Do you have the answers that could help someone else? Use that as your motivation to do something. Here is the story of my entrepreneurial journey.

There were no business owners or entrepreneurs in my immediate or extended family. I grew up being told to "make an honest living." This meant, generally, to finish high school, find a job, find a wife, have children, and follow my destiny to live in suburbia. Earning six-figures seemed so far beyond reality, something that was only reserved for wealthy people. This average lifestyle just never really appealed me. I grew up in a lower-middle class neighborhood in a tiny house. Every home I grew up in, my parents bought as a basket-case fixer-upper that we would remodel over time. My family always took great pride in anything we had, even when we had little. I suppose this instilled in me my habit of looking at the potential in things. I look beyond how something just appears at the moment. I've carried that belief into looking for classic cars that need restoration, and when looking at people that I can help bring to a higher level. I am an optimist; I always try to see the potential in others.

Despite my humble beginnings, I was never blind to what existed outside of my immediate environment. My neighborhood was older, but it was surrounded by some much nicer neighborhoods. My hometown of Friendswood, Texas was one of the more affluent suburbs of Houston, with an excellent school system. That was the reason my parents moved us there, so that my sister and I could get a good education. As a kid, I'd ride my bicycle through nicer neighborhoods, and dream about what it must be like to live in one of those bigger homes. Seeing people with extra cars in the driveway just seemed so far away from my reality. But, I had evidence that this more extravagant lifestyle existed, and I knew that I wanted it. I was hungry.

I'm fortunate enough to still remember the very first time the light bulb came on for me in terms of scalability and earning millions. I was watching TV with my mom in the early 1980s as a pre-teen. I can't recall the exact show, but it was some afternoon talk show with featured guests. There was a silly looking Japanese man as the guest on the show. He was wearing a white shirt with a bunch of colorful rubber octopuses sewed to it. My mom is Japanese, so we were both curious about this guy. This man was Ken "Dr. Fad" Hakuta, the inventor of the popular "Wacky Wall-Walker" toys of that era. These were very sticky octopuses that you threw against the wall, and they'd slowly tumble down the wall. These toys were on every store counter, in every gumball machine, and in every cereal box as a prize. I even had a few of them. As we listened to the interview, I heard him say that he sold 200 million of them. Even though they only sold for about a dollar apiece, this guy was a multi-millionaire because of this idea. That vision of scalability has always stuck with me.

I wanted a new skateboard and a new bike. No company would hire me at age 11, so I figured out how to earn money. My dad gave me permission to push our lawnmower around the neighborhood and knock on doors. I charged $10 to mow the front and back yards. I'd balance the metal fuel can on top of the engine, and push that mower from house to house, to any that seemed to need a trim. If they declined my mowing offer, I'd ask if I could wash their car for them. I usually got one, sometimes both gigs. Recurring revenue! I started to have repeat customers on a weekly basis. Trust me, I hated mowing yards. But, what other choice did I have? Complaining wouldn't get me a bike. Some of the other kids in the neighborhood thought it was weird that I wanted to work. I bought that bike and many other toys.

There have been numerous things that I've done to monetize my skills along the way. This lasted even through most of my 20s before I started actual companies. I've done things such as installing car stereo systems and alarms in the driveway. Detailing cars. Building woodworking projects. Flipping purchases. Small hand-built inventions. Automotive photography. Freelance magazine journalism. University newspaper illustration. I even hand-drew signs and flyers for local businesses before the digital age arrived. If I could teach myself something and earn income from it, I did it. I've always been wired this way, and I still am.

I got my first real job at age 15 when McDonald's discovered our small town. I worked there over 2 years during high school. While I don't recommend working at a fast food restaurant, I will tell you I found some value there that most probably didn't even notice. I learned how an efficient process for every aspect of a business can greatly improve the business. We had a defined process for every single task, every single product. There was a separate VHS video for every single process to train employees. Everything at McDonald's was about time efficiency and earning money. There was an emphasis on workflow, timing, portion control, consistency, and repeatability. While co-workers were just thinking it was some crappy minimum-wage job, I was taking mental notes on everything. There is a reason that McDonald's grew exponentially. It wasn't because of the food's tastiness. Marketing, branding, and efficiency rule the domain.

I was the first person in my family to graduate from college. I attended the University of Houston. It was a struggle, and some of the worst times of my life were during that period. I was essentially a walking zombie, suffering from constant sleep deprivation. I paid for college myself while working full-time. Engineering school was much more difficult than high school. While I earned A's and graduated in the top 10% in high school, I suddenly found myself as a C student, barely making average grades in college. The stress of the studies and being broke really put me through the paces. To make things worse, I was driving an unreliable Nissan that was 10 years old, and it would occasionally leave me stranded roadside. It was all I could afford, and I had to fix it myself when it broke. I share this to illustrate that I wasn't some genius that had everything figured out. Not even close.

In 2000, our country was facing another economic recession, and I was laid off from my job. I had no savings, and I had to survive off of credit cards for several months. This really put me into debt, and things really hit a financial and mental low for me. I had a newborn son and a failed relationship with his mother. I have no doubt that I was in a deep depression for over a year, as I don't seem to have much memory of that period of my life. All I could do was work wherever and whenever I could. I repaired cars, waited tables, and minimized expenses. My small apartment felt more like a prison cell since I couldn't even afford to leave it to do anything. I continued to teach myself new skills in hopes of monetizing them. I learned how to program html to create websites. I learned Adobe Photoshop and Illustrator. I started messing with graphic design and creating basic websites. I cold-called hundreds of small businesses that needed websites, and I began building websites for them. Eventually, the recession evaporated, and I had another job, newfound skills, and more side-hustles. It took me three years to unbury myself from all that debt.

In November 2001, a car friend and I started an online community for performance cars. This creation was a result of doing something better than what existed. We were members on another car forum which suffered from being unreliable. We grew tired of how that other site was mismanaged, so we created our own. Our website LS1Tech.com surpassed the competitor in only 2 short years in terms of member count and revenue. Our website community grew into the largest GM based website on the internet in only a few more years. At the peak of our ownership, we had 150 paying advertiser accounts, and the site traffic averaged 100,000 unique visitors per day. Even GM advertised with us. Today, that online community has nearly 300,000 registered members.

This business was an exercise in scalability, branding, and marketing. There was no social media back then, so we grew the site organically by networking and advertising. We'd have car parts and gift certificate giveaways to encourage people to sign up. We'd reach out and cold-email or call potential advertisers found in magazines. My business partner John and I would work on this website almost nightly for the first two years. We had no idea of the potential, as our goals were originally set much lower. We simply blew past goals all the time. Looking back at the sale of the company in 2007, we just did so many things right in terms of valuation. We had years of documented revenue, an astoundingly high profit margin, well-defined processes, a recurring revenue business model, minimal operating budget requirements, a positive cash flow business model, unique branding, and no full-time employees. This side-hustle turned both of us into millionaires while we both had full-time professional careers. Even today, this still seems crazy to have been a part of.

No matter where you came from or what you currently know, just understand that the potential for success exists for those willing to work for it. Nothing worth having comes easily. You have to set goals so that you do not wander around aimlessly. Once goals are established, it becomes easier to identify the necessary steps to reach those goals. Without goals, you are basically lost without a map. You have no destination identified. There is no get-rich-quick, there is only discipline, consistency, and patience. With a goal in mind, you can use it to determine every key decision in your life. Each time you arrive at a fork in the road, your goal will serve to highlight the proper direction. Which decision moves you closer to your goals? Which moves you further away from them? Which path will you decide?

The most important message? Get started.

"Fear and confidence are both imaginary. You simply decide which one to live with."

Tony Whatley, Hopeful Best-Selling Author

RESOURCES

I have a dedicated page on my website for sharing the most updated resources to help you on your entrepreneurial journey. I list useful books, podcasts, software, and information that will help you with your business. Please visit www.365driven.com and look for "resources" on the menu. I'd also love to hear from you! It would be a great honor if you could share this book with your friends, and leave me an online review from wherever you purchased it. It would mean the world to me. I hope this book helps you find your own definition of success.

Sincerely,
Tony Whatley

Find me online:

www.365driven.com
Facebook.com/365driven
Instagram.com/365driven

Made in the USA
San Bernardino, CA
06 February 2019